More Memories from the Marshes

More Memories from

the Marshes

People of the Broads, Past and Present

Margaret Dye

Dedicated to Christopher Cadbury C.B.E. in recognition of all his achievements for the people and quiet places of Broadland.

The Larks Press

Published by the Larks Press
Ordnance Farmhouse, Guist Bottom, Dereham
NR20 5PF

April 1996

British Library Cataloguing-in-Publication-Data
A Catalogue record for this book is available from the British Library.

The author and publishers wish to thank all those who have kindly
allowed their photographs to be used for this book.

Printed by the Lanceni Press, Fakenham, Norfolk.

Introduction

My last booklet, *Memories of Mill & Marsh,* was written in a mood of rage and despair. By the middle of this century it seemed that Broadland had reached a crisis point. The slow deterioration of habitat and species over the years was due to several causes:-

Drainage of the marshes to increase agricultural land.

Over-zealous use of fertilisers, pesticides and herbicides by Broadland farmers.

Discharge of phosphate-rich effluent from sewage works.

Discharge of factory wastes into the river system.

Decline in dyke maintenance.

Eutrophication of the Broads became evident after years of the leaching out of agricultural chemicals. Growth of algae due to the enrichment of the waterways resulted in the dying back of water plants. Thus food chains were affected. Examples are numerous. Here are two:- Winter reed bed declined, followed by an impoverishment of invertebrate life. In 1955-56 tufted duck wintering on Hickling Broad numbered 160 and this number decreased to 31 between 1976-79.

Drainage of Broadland marshes meant that the natural feeding grounds of the marsh harrier and waders over-wintering on the Broads decreased. Swampy areas and reed beds deteriorated, so the bittern, relying on such habitats, declined in numbers. Michael Seago's county-wide survey of the booming male bittern recorded sixty in 1954. By 1994 nationwide only 16 booming bitterns were noted.

Broadland wetlands are unique in Europe, yet all I read about was how well the Dutch were managing their habitats, and how rapidly Norfolk's were decaying. During 1993/4 my longing to hold on to the past and prevent further decline, made me sail around waterways collecting stories and life-styles of river craftsmen. *Memories of Mill and Marsh* was published. But you cannot hold on to the past and I began to find comfort in the slow realisation that a good future can be built on a sound past. My interviews taught me that the sons and daughters of the past generation felt equally passionately about their environment, and many thought quality of life meant staying in Broadland carrying on traditional crafts rather than seeking better-paid work in the faster lane of commuter life-styles.

Hopefully there will be a balance between local workers and academic and business people coming into the area to promote and develop economic and tourism possibilities within the area.

Since East Anglia is the fastest growing region in the UK, predicted to continue to be so well into the next century, one must have confidence that the decline in Broadland has been researched and documented with strategies implemented to halt, reverse and finance these policies.

One can see many hopeful signs. In 1989 the Broads Authority became responsible for navigation, recreation, conservation and planning throughout Broadland and it is now active in many aspects relating to the better management of this newest National Park which has more than 125 miles (250km) of waterways, acres of flat open marshland, and misty woodland linking medieval and modern villages and towns. Broads information centres have been set up at Beccles, Ranworth, Ludham, Hoveton and Norwich and far-sighted and hugely expensive plans made to improve water quality and halt bank erosion. Ideas to introduce slower boat speeds, adopting less damaging boat hull design, and to encourage holiday-makers to switch to renting electric-powered boats, are all ideas that should show results. Many organisations such as Eastern Electricity, the Norfolk Wildlife Trust, the Soap and Detergent Industry Environmental Trust, the University of East Anglia, the Broads Society, the National Rivers Authority and many others are helping in the work of cleaning up Broadland and, even more important, financing apprentices and training centres which will ensure that the future workforce is well informed and competent.

It is rewarding to have watched this continuing cycle. I was learning to sail in the 1950s when sail on the Broads was beginning to decline, with holiday and motor craft growing in demand. Customers wanted more comfort afloat, and so cruisers were designed with bluff bows, broad beams, and square sterns. Now, in the 1990s, financial encouragement is give to owners restoring Broadland classic sailing yachts, and boat shapes that should cause minimum wash and less bank erosion are being designed. In the 1950s petrol was the fuel used to power the hire fleets, and spillage soon evaporated, but diesel fuel which has replaced it caused other pollutions. A movement is now under way to encourage the use of electric power in hire boats. Detergents at boatyards are being replaced by detergent-free soap powders and heavy fines and prosecution threats given to yards who cause diesel oil spillages, and to sportsmen who use lead shot as they hunt and fish the Broadland area.

Norfolk is in no danger of becoming a county museum which fossilises and trades on its past, and so *Wanderbug* and I sail around looking forward into the past; we realise that the old life-styles of wildfowling, eel catching, hand reed-cutting and mowing the marshes for hay, are gone for ever, but Norfolk still offers an increasing number of people an attractive life-style, timeless holidays in a peaceful area and a thriving business culture, given its close proximity to Europe.

Just as John Loynes, pioneer of the boat hiring business at the beginning of this century, discovered that the best way to explore the Broads was by using a half-decker with a tilt to sleep beneath at nights, so *Wanderbug* and I enjoy living afloat and talking to Broadland people as we sail this marvellous waterland of mysterious, misty landscapes. In by-gone days the bittern boomed and bred in this area and George Christopher Davies wrote that 'Surlingham Broad was so chocked with bream and roach that at spawning time the water appeared as a moving mass of fish.' So I hope to hear the bittern booming again as I produce *More Memories from the Marshes*, because eventually boat numbers will be controlled, boat speed reduced, and all landowners, conservationists, farmers, shooting and fishing enthusiasts, and holiday-makers will work together to understand and establish a better future for Broadland.

Margaret Dye
1996

A map of the Broads may be found on page 38

Contents

Christopher Cadbury

Conservationist

'I'm going to see Mr Cadbury.' I explained, apologising for using Hickling Sailing Club's slipway as they prepared for their summer regatta. One of the committee members, busily rigging his boat said, 'He is our vice-president. He has been very good to the club.' I was to hear that remark many more times.

Enjoying Hickling Broad, swathed in a heat haze during the hottest July on record, was a delight. Many times I had seen Whiteslea Lodge with its beautifully-thatched roof peering over the reed beds, as I passed down the Broad along Heigham Sound. Today I rowed along the private dyke where Arthur Beales was waiting to tie my dinghy alongside *Meadowsweet*. I was shown a duck punt moored in a boatshed close by. 'She was probably the last one Jimmy Turner built,' said Mr Cadbury 'and she was modelled on the one Jim Vincent used earlier in the century.' ('A first class gun punt has very subtle lines and can only be built properly by the most intelligent of boatwrights', said A. H. Emerson many years ago.) 'Oh for the golden days when the water was so clear and the bottom so hard for quanting...' had been a comment made in an earlier letter from Mr Cadbury.

Meadowsweet, built by Waldro Beales another local boatbuilder, had been hired by Mr Cadbury, when, as a young man living in Norwich, he worked as a travelling salesman in the family business. Now she is owned by Mr Cadbury and the family enjoy sailing her on the Broad.

Whiteslea Lodge had been the family home since Mr Cadbury had bought it from Lord Desborough at the suggestion of the warden Jim Vincent in1944. The site was given to the Norfolk Naturalists' Trust (an organisation established in 1922) and it was designated a National Nature Reserve shortly afterwards. 'I was almost entirely responsible for the reserve, working with Mr Bassett Horner, the Trust's Estate Agent, for many years until we set up a management committee consisting of representatives of the Norfolk Naturalists' Trust and the Council of Nature - of which I am still the chairman. Arthur Beales has worked on the estate since 1945, and now that he has retired, he is my wonderful caretaker of the Lodge', explained Mr Cadbury in a letter shortly before we met. Honor Cottage, named in

1

memory of Mr Cadbury's first wife, is one of the homes provided for the estate workers and enjoyed by Mr Beales.

Sitting outside Whiteslea, I was shown the lawn patched by Mr Beales. The land has dropped 20 inches, and the quay-heading has been repaired after the very wet winter of 1993/4. Flooding has always been a problem too. Mr Cadbury explained how the drainage had been re-designed, the Lodge shored up and the land restored to its original level.

'Where have all the swallows gone? They went so early this year,' mused Mr Cadbury as he saw me admiring the new thatch, completed by the Aldred brothers last spring. 'Have the invertebrates disappeared, are the food chains for waders broken down?' He then went on to enthuse about his latest idea - to get better aeration into the waterpools that he had dug out in the 1950s and 60s bringing back the invertebrates which would then entice the birds to return. With modern educational awareness, Mr Cadbury explained that he wanted to create a walkway for school children around the reserve, with bird tables and a pond, but avoiding sensitive areas. 'It is easy to mix plants and people,' he said, 'but more difficult to let children roam freely on the bird feeding and nesting areas. In one marsh behind the Lodge 30 years ago I recorded 22 different nests but there were few visitors in those days'.

Whiteslea Lodge with *Meadowsweet* **moored alongside**

It was incredibly peaceful sitting beside the Lodge on that hot summer day. Mr Cadbury, his spare figure, open-air complexion, warm smile and eyes sparkling with enthusiasm which belied his eighty odd years, told me about his early friendship with Jim Vincent. 'It was Silver Jubilee Day, 1935, one of the best birding days I ever had at Hickling; I saw spoonbills, both godwits, grey plover, dusky redshanks and black terns on Rush Hills, all in full breeding plumage, and was shown nests of bittern, marsh harrier, Montague's harrier, short-eared owl and bearded tit'.

Christopher Cadbury's ability to relate to the workers of the estate struck me most forcefully. On the mantelpiece of the Lodge lounge were photographs of all the past estate wardens. 'Mr Cadbury has been very good to us' was a comment several of them made to me. Mr Beales worked on the estate as marsh foreman until he retired, and now acts as Mr Cadbury's caretaker to Whiteslea, and there were many indications of his loyalty, even affection, for his work. Freshly cut flowers from his garden were arranged in Whiteslea's dining room. Mr George Bishop, a previous warden, much loved by everybody, also showed affection and loyalty. One man said to Mr Cadbury 'I look on you as my father '. Mr Cadbury said 'I seem to get on with the men well'. Betty Spooner, a village lady, greatly travelled and well-read, told me 'Mr Cadbury is a very kind man, a Quaker. He has quietly helped so many people.' And she mentioned Mr Piggin, a senior marshman under Jim Vincent, who later became warden, as just one example. 'We always interview the wives of prospective workers of the Hickling reserve, because if they are happy, everything works well,' explained Mr Cadbury.

'This place has been a bird paradise for sixty years,' said Mr Cadbury with a hint of pride. However, as a home there were small drawbacks, because, regularly each winter in the early years, it flooded. Mr Cadbury remembers skating down the corridors of his home, and the legs of the chairs on which we were sitting bore watermarks many inches high. 'Somebody must be looking after us,' remarked a smiling Mr Cadbury. 'I rang Arthur last week (in October) saying 'you can take up the carpets, now all the family have gone away'. So the following day the carpets were rolled up. Next day the severe '93 autumn floods came unexpectedly early!'

Returning again to a topic uppermost in Mr Cadbury's thoughts, the visual deterioration of the environment, he said, 'Where have all the birds gone? When Stuart Linsell was warden here, he recorded many breeding

3

snipe, little tern, ringed plover, avocets, oystercatchers and many other vanished breeding birds, nesting on the reserve. House-martins used to walk above our heads as we lay in bed. They went when gloss paint was used on the lodge, but they are back now; and they seem to enjoy renting their council homes.' Smilingly Mr Cadbury pointed to the artificial papier-mâché nests that he had erected beneath the thatch.

Mr Cadbury came to Norfolk quite by chance. His family firm could easily have sent him to Bradford or Halifax, but in the 1930s the grandson of the Bourn-ville family firm came to sell cocoa and chocolate around Norfolk. Successful as a salesman, he also grew to love Norfolk people and places. His success has spread far beyond the

Christopher Cadbury C.B.E., 1908-1995, on one of his reserves

family firm. Over thirty nature sites have have been purchased by Christopher Cadbury and donated to the nation. The early purchases were 350 acres of Weeting Heath at £3 an acre which, together with Hickling, became the first two National Nature Reserves in Britain in the `40s. 'Weeting is a top site for rare birds, plants, lichens and invertebrates, and some 6,000 people annually visit to see the stone curlews,' remarked Mr Cadbury with quiet enthusiasm.

Other sites too he told me about, with justifiable pride: one in Devon, another in Cornwall, one in Kent, another in Scotland, and one in the Falklands. 'There's one in the Seychelles,' said Mr Cadbury, 'a tropical island, with everything. There are no rats there, hence the huge bird population with many of them ground-nesting all the year round, but all tropical islands have tourists and poachers; the trick is to get the balance right. I seem to have an eye for what places are worth protecting.' Mr Cadbury is hopeful

4

that Hickling Reserve may be nursed back to better health. He said, 'The pre-war Broads idyll is now a sepia memory; then there were few boats and the water was crystal clear; you could see fish and vegetation on the bottom and it was solid and you could walk across it. But then it was dredged to accommodate the bigger boats and they cut through the clay and the peat was churned up and a thick sediment established. Phosphates and nitrates washing off the fields have created the pea soup water which Broadland knows today. The eels have largely gone - another break in the bittern's food chain.'

Christopher Cadbury is a very busy man and he still travels widely. He is the last surviving member of the Norfolk Trust Council which he attended from 1944 under the chairmanship of Russell Colman, Timothy Colman's grandfather. Also he is the longest serving Trust councillor of the present 48 councillors, many of whom he helped to launch. Benefiting from his organising and money-creating gifts are many educational, historical trusts and technological organisations.

Before leaving, I was given a glimpse inside Whiteslea which I shall always remember. Rowing away across Hickling Broad, I had time to consider what I had previously read about Christopher Cadbury whom I had found such an energetic, enthusiastic and modest man:- 'A leader of our time', said Lawrence Rich, editor of the National Trust magazine. 'His genius was in recognising an important wild life habitat and bringing it under the Trust's protection. ... For over 50 years Christopher Cadbury has not only stood head and shoulders above the rest in nature conservation, but in many respects, he has actually shaped it.'

This article was written before the death of Christopher Cadbury in 1995.

Jim Vincent

Warden of Hickling

'His knowledge was encyclopaedic' said Lord Templewood. 'One of the finest personalities in Broadland' was another tribute paid to Jim Vincent on his death in 1944.

Jim Vincent lived at Hickling and, apart from a period when he served as ground crew with the Royal Flying Corps at Great Yarmouth during the First World War, he rarely left his village. Born in 1884 he was the fifth child and first son of Robert Vincent who was a professional eelcatcher and wildfowler. Rumour has it that an upturned boat was Robert's home for one period in his life! To help in bringing up a large family Bob was able to take advantage of the free fishing and shooting around Hickling Broad at that time. Cash for collecting the eggs of rare birds would also have afforded him extra income. Jim followed in his father's footsteps (his brother William born in 1885 was drowned after falling through the ice whilst retrieving coot shot by his father).

By the age of sixteen Jim was an expert at identifying birds. His knowledge of the area's wildlife was so extensive that he was recommended to a Cambridge undergraduate visiting the area, the Hon. Edwin Montague who was an enthusiastic bird and egg collector. Their meeting began a 20-year friendship, and it transformed Jim's life from agricultural labour on farms, with the possibility of training for the Methodist Ministry, to that of a keeper.

Edwin Montague joined with Lord Lucas and Sir Edward Grey to form a syndicate to rent Whiteslea Lodge Estate at Hickling because they enjoyed shooting ducks and coot. Jim Vincent was employed to look after their sporting venture and bird sanctuary. In 1909 with wages of £1.10s a week and a rent-free cottage, he married a local schoolteacher. Jim and Ruth had two children. There was no electricity and no sanitation in their cottage. Candles, oil lamps and a coal stove supplied their needs until the house was modernised in the 1930s.

Travelling the three miles to work from the Pleasure Boat to Whiteslea Lodge by punt, also ferrying guests to the Lodge by boat, Jim made the most of his opportunities to observe the wildlife all around him. During winter

Jim and Ruth Vincent

months, Jim would have worked from 8.00 a.m. to 4.00 p.m., but in the spring and summer he would have been out on the estate all hours. Once in May 1913 he stayed out all night to see a snowy owl that had been reported in the Horsey area.

Jim and the syndicate renting Whiteslea Lodge discovered that their policy of cutting, grazing and flooding the area was paying dividends. In 1910 the Montagu's harrier began to re-colonise the upper Thurne reed beds. They had previously bred in that area in 1883. When Jim discovered the first nest, he arranged to have a hide positioned and a full-time watch kept on the nest. In the following years he found the first bittern near Sutton Broad. No bitterns had been known to nest in Broadland since 1886.

More birds, and more guests at Whiteslea Lodge to enjoy these flourishing marshes, reed beds and meadows, resulted from Jim Vincent's work. A large painted frieze showing all the birds recorded at Hickling, executed by a famous local bird artist, Roland Green, is one of the lovely reminders of Whiteslea when kings, city gentry and nobility enjoyed The Lodge.

In 1911 Edwin Montague persuaded Jim Vincent to keep a diary. He did this daily until his untimely death in 1944. Years later, when Montague was a minister in the Asquith government, he decided to organise the pre-servation of Jim's diary. Over two hundred birds were recorded and so he commissioned G. E. Lodge R.A., a famous Edwardian bird artist, to illustrate the diary. Extracts from this diary give a flavour of his unique book:-1911, 'June 11th - Found the fourth Montagu's nest in Horsey with two eggs...August 17th - Saw the Marsh Harrier on Whiteslea, Sandmartins and Swallows are roosting in the reeds by thousands on Hickling and Heigham Sounds at night... 'Oct. 28th - Nudd & I saw a beautiful snow bunting near Pleasure Island. It is one of the best I have ever seen.'

As keeper, Jim Vincent's contribution to the Hickling area was to establish habitats for birds to over-winter or for migrating spring and summer birds, and to provide birds for the shooting parties. Mr Montague and his friends were determined to establish a bird paradise at Hickling as well as a sporting estate. Jim recorded 247 different species of birds, and he studied to provide them with habitats that would ensure their breeding success. For example, he realized that harriers liked rough reedbeds, bitterns and bearded tits needed thin reed beds, whilst wagtails and plovers enjoyed the dry grass of the marshlands.

Jim Vincent was a pioneer of bird ringing. As a result he found out the migratory pattern of the wild mallard and discovered that there was movement from S.E. to the E, and towards N. & N.E. in late autumn, and back again the following spring across the narrowest bit of the North Sea. His observations made him one of the great ornithologists of his time. He organised coot shoots and participants included King George VI, George Lodge and Sir Peter Scott. A record was achieved by seventeen guns on February 10th 1934:-

     1,213 coot, 14 pochard duck, 1 shoveler duck,
     10 mallard duck, 24 mute swan, 7 tufted duck, 2 moorhens.

The village people of Hickling were supplied with the birds after the shoots. Skinned coot were rich in protein, and many people still recall that their favourite dish in those days was coot stew. Jim's son, Ivor, told me he used to be given five shillings each time he quanted the gentry out to the butts (hides) in the broads, and he recalls cycling round the village to distribute the coot to each household in Hickling village. He also remembered that after the coot shoots big parties would be held at the

Lodge. One day a peach pie was put outside on the water-butt to cool, but the dogs ate it before it could be placed on the dining table to be enjoyed by the city guests!

Whiteslea flooded regularly during winter and spring tides. The Lodge rested on boggy land, its base merely fortified with faggots. As these rotted away, the building subsided. Staying there in October 1927, Lord Desborough stepped out of bed into six inches of water. Shortly after that, a massive building programme shored up the building.

Edwin Vincent helping at the coot shoot

Edwin, Jim's elder son, using the first year of his father's diaries, produced a book *A Season of Birds*. Ivor, Jim's younger son presented the entire diaries for 1912-1944, totalling thirty, to Norwich Castle Museum in memory of his parents. Christopher Cadbury said of Jim Vincent, 'He was a great friend of mine, and it was through him that I was able to purchase Hickling for the Norfolk Trust from Lord Desborough', and he wrote to Ivor Vincent in 1986 saying 'the diaries and scrapbooks provide fascinating glimpses of bird population and changes in the area. If the wind directions and strengths recorded daily could be computerised they would give valuable information . ..'

9

Not only was Jim a natural gamekeeper, he was also a good sailor, who was well-placed in the annual Hickling summer regatta. He was also an outstanding game and clay pigeon shot, winning the Daily Telegraph Sporting Championship Cup in 1933. He was a fine fisherman, and he used to visit schools to enthuse the young about this sport. He also broadcast and lectured on wildfowling. The Royal Society for the Protection of Birds presented him with a Gold Medal.

In 1930 Jim was invited to stay at Sandringham for three days shooting. His host, King George V, asked him what he thought of Sandringham. Jim replied, 'Your Majesty, if heaven is only half as good as Sandringham that will be good enough for me.'

Ivor Vincent in a butt (hide) on Hickling Broad, 1936

Mrs Gwen Amis

Proprietor of the Pleasure Boat Inn

Gwen Amis was born in 1910. Her Norfolk-born father married a Devonshire girl. Together they took over the Pleasure Boat Inn in 1914 when Gwen was a toddler. Gwen's childhood contained memories of school days at the local Hickling school, where boys were caned (on their bottoms!) for carrying mice into the classroom and letting them out during lessons, of being a Brownie and then a Girl Guide, of the company going to London to compete in country dancing and team games, and coming third in the country. 'The Sunday School outing was a highlight,' reminisced Mrs Amis. 'We went to Palling to spend a happy day, being taken there by horse-drawn wagons loaned by farmers.'

Another childhood memory was the annual summer tea party for about one hundred and fifty children given by Lord and Lady Desborough who spent a great deal of time at Whiteslea Lodge during July and August. Lady Desborough was Lady-in-Waiting to Queen Mary and so would have spent much of the season in London.

The Pleasure Boat Inn about 1900

Gwen remembers earning 1/2d. a bundle for peeling osiers on a willow farm. Each bundle took about half-an-hour to prepare, and baskets were woven from them. 'It was good pocket money' said Gwen. She also earned 10 shillings weekly, because together with her brother, she helped her mother run the Pleasure Boat public house while her father was away on active service during the First World War.

At the early age of fourteen years Gwen became a member of the village W. I. as her mother was then president of the Institute. To make money for the Institute the village people bought a pig which one of the members kept in her garden; everyone took turns to feed it. Eventually the pig was sold to a butcher, 'and what pork it was!' said Gwen some sixty years after.

Gwen recalled how her mother was paid 2s 6d. per person to provide lunches on the wherry moored on Hickling Broad during the annual August regatta. Lunch consisted of roast leg of pork, silverside of beef, salads, trifles, and cheese for the contestants sailing half deckers and punts. That was in 1924, and now, seventy years on, the Hickling Sailing Club is thriving, filling the Broad with a variety of sailing craft every summer Sunday.

In 1924 Gwen's family moved out of the Pleasure Boat and built a boarding house with six letting bedrooms, providing accommodation for visitors who came to the village to sail, shoot and fish. In those days the Broad used to freeze over for several weeks at a time and skating became a popular pastime with young and old in the villages. On one such occasion a Dr Bell drove a pony and trap over the ice. The ice gave way, and the half-drowned pony was dragged into the waterside public house where a bottle of rum was poured down his throat. According to Gwen the pony collapsed and fell fast asleep at the bar.

One Christmas Eve a ship was driven ashore at Palling beach. Gwen and two boys collected the cargo of oranges, lying all over the beach covered in oil. After cleaning they were distributed around the village.

During the First World War the Broads area was banned to all except those living in the villages. Seaplanes landed on the slipway at Hickling during this time. Five officers came to dismantle one and they stayed at the Pleasure Boat Inn. One sent a piano after his stay there, and the piano was a centre of attraction to those elderly locals who were not involved in active war service and to the retired wherrymen and fishermen who used the pub as their focal point in the evenings.

Summer days on Hickling Broad with the artist, Roland Green, 1927

Gwen married in 1935 and she returned to the Pleasure Boat Inn to run it with her husband. When he was away serving in the Second World War, she continued single-handed. 'Life was hard' Gwen admitted. 'Rationing made life difficult - the beer came in on a Thursday and was all gone by Sunday.' However, Mrs Amis was just as involved with village community service as she had been as a child, and also found time to run the local ambulance service. 'I attended seven crashed aircraft around here. Two nights we were in Norwich, and we went to the bombing of Horning Swan. A plane once crashed on land in Stubb Road. With the help of the police we found the men on Palling road, carrying their parachutes, because they had all baled out successfully. We took them to the searchlight site where they had a meal before going back to base' said Mrs Amis. 'We ran a `welcome home' fund for the men and women serving in the war. Once we had an auction with items such as sheets, farm butter, and day-old chickens. With the sum raised, over £200, we were able to send our people £2 10s each.

On an August Bank holiday Monday, soldiers were sorting out detonators in the village hall at Sea Palling. Tragically the hall was blown up. Gwen and her helpers were given bags and asked to pick up the bodies. She found a ginger scalp! The following week they were called to a mined beach at Waxham - two children had been blown in half.

After the war, Gwen's husband returned; trade at the pub improved.

Lunches, teas and wedding receptions were catered for. Although Mr and Mrs Amis had no children of their own, not only did Gwen help in bringing up her brother's children, but she also brought up a friend's three children for five war years, when they were evacuated from London. During the 1953 floods, the men in the pub were asked to fill sandbags to help the sea defences at Sea Palling. Gwen joined in. One man said 'Missus, you are filling those bags like an old woman.' 'I am an old woman' she retorted shovelling away.

Mr Amis died in the early 1950s, but Gwen carried on living and working at the Pleasure Boat. She only retired from there after a total of thirty-seven years. Gwen said 'I have had a wonderful life, catering for various functions from Darts Club suppers to entertaining Royalty, including the Duke of Edinburgh, Prince Charles, Lord Brabourn, Viscount and Lady Allenbrook, the Earl of Leicester and Sir R. Adean. Others included the Lord Mayor of London, Richard Todd, Evelyn Laye and Muriel Pavlow. I had an arrangement with the syndicate of Whiteslea Lodge that if it got waterlogged in the winter, they could use my rooms.'

When Prince Charles was twelve years old, his father and the royal party came to shoot coot. 'They wanted supper of Norfolk steak-and-kidney pie' recalled Gwen. The first evening the men were at the bar when the high jinks of the children, engaged in a pillow fight in the bedroom above the bar, became very audible and hectic. Mrs Amis went upstairs and ordered the young prince back into bed, with the Duke of Edinburgh at her elbow maintaining a strict discipline.

In 1971 Mrs Amis retired from business life and now she lives in a bungalow close by the Pleasure Boat. 'I wouldn't want to go anywhere else' she said. Her involvement with village life is as great as ever, whether it be the Women's Institute or the Hickling Sailing Club, Age Concern or the Nature Trail hut.

On the walls of her bungalow are rosettes showing her success in local shows for jams and pickles, also photographs of her `adopted' children in their university robes. Her scrapbooks are full of events. in which she has taken part, in local drama, choirs, and charity events during her busy life. 'I'm a jack of all trades' said Gwen who, now handicapped with arthritis, knits mittens and socks and shawls for the disadvantaged in the war-stricken zones in Europe. 'I just like to be out and about, and I love to organise.'

Duke and Charles flooded out

ws Chronicle Reporters

NOW and ice covered almost all Britain last night, floods threatened much of the rest—and the weather forecast was: More blizzards to come.

Standby warnings had gone out to R.A.F. helicopter teams to be ready for food and fodder-dropping flights over cut-off villages.

Floods have already struck the Norfolk Broads as the Duke of Edinburgh and the Prince of Wales discovered.

They arrived at Hickling Broad on Friday for the annual coot shoot there, only to find that the luxurious Whiteslea Lodge prepared for them had been flooded.

To the inn

So the royal party called at the little Pleasure Boat Inn, and asked for rooms.

The Pleasure Boat has only four rooms to let. The Duke and Prince moved in, and Mrs. Gwen Amis, the landlord's wife, prepared their meal.

They stayed for two nights. As local farmworkers and boatbuilders came for their pint and darts, the royal party were having their evening meal in the little dining-room.

Said Mrs. Amis last night after her visitors had driven back to Sandringham: " Our usual customers came and went as they pleased the whole time

" Before he left the Duke thanked me."

Elsewhere in Britain freezing roads after a day of blizzards caused the A.A. to appeal to motorists to drive cautiously this morning.

Express Staff Reporter

PRINCE PHILIP and the Prince of Wales drove to Sandringham yesterday after being "marooned" for two nights in a fishermen's inn.

They arrived at the village of Hickling, in Norfolk, on Friday evening to take part in the annual coot shoot on Hickling Broad.

It was intended that they should put up at Whiteslea Lodge, a luxurious thatched bungalow on a reedy island in the middle of the 400-acre lake.

But the water had risen so high that the bungalow was flooded.

So Prince Philip's party called at the Pleasure Boat Inn, on the edge of the broad.

Fifty-year-old landlord Albert Amis and his wife Gwen, aged 48, were asked : " Can you put us up ? "

Pints and darts

Landlord Amis knew that if the lodge was flooded he would be asked to put up the party and he said last night :—

" I was having a cup of tea at about 4.30 p.m. when Prince Philip and the Prince of Wales arrived.

" We had not expected them until two hours later, and Major Aubrey Buxton, who organised the shoot, was not in to receive them.

" But everything was ready for the guests, however, and we made tea for them.

" Electric heaters were already on, and a fire was burning in my private lounge, which was placed at the Duke's disposal."

Landlord Albert fixed up his visitors while his wife got busy in the kitchen.

Prince Philip had a room to himself. The Prince of Wales shared his room with two other boys—one the son of Major Buxton.

AT the edge of a sheltered creek near Wroxham stands a remote little inn that has quietly become the most informal haunt of English royalty.

Just a country pub. But round the merry log fire of The Pleasure Boat at Hickling Broad, Norfolk, princes have warmed themselves in simple comfort.

Here I met the landlord's wife with a royal secret.

Gwen Amis, cheerful and dark-haired, appeared from the kitchen with a huge tray of steaming potatoes baked in their jackets. Rugged sportsmen in thick pullovers and thigh-length waders quickly crowded round.

"The Duke of Edinburgh

THE Pleasure Boat Inn at Hickling Broad where the Duke of Edinburgh and Charles stayed for two nights. "Our usual customers came and went as they pleased the whole time," said the landlord's wife

---

King George VI

King George VI. took part in a coot shoot a short time before he died. On that occasion Mr. Amis was the fourth gun away from him.

The shoot takes place on the mile-square broad itself, the guns going out in punts which are quanted. Contrary to a widely-held belief that the coot is not edible, Hickling people have always regarded them as an excellent dish.

The Pleasure Boat, a Bullard's house, is one of the most famous of the Broadland inns and is known to thousands of holidaymakers.

At this time of the year many pike fishermen stay there. But there were no other guests last week-end.

GWEN KEEPS A ROYAL SECRET

Gwen behind the bar

has been here several times," Gwen confided above the chatter, "but we never tell anyone, or make a fuss. People come to Hickling for peace and not to be pestered."

Royal visitors to The Pleasure Boat can be sure this businesslike woman will defend their privacy.

She considers information on the subject too be top secret.

After she had brought me food and drink, Gwen went to the door to say goodbye to her husband, Alfred, and a schoolboy nephew, Graham, who were leaving with the other men to hunt wildfowl.

One crisp morning last year she had watched another schoolboy set out, excitedly, on a similar adventure. That boy was Prince Charles. He was making the shooting trip with his father.

The boy prince had arrived at the inn with the Duke after they were flooded out of the island bungalow where they had been staying.

Hurriedly, Mrs. Amis prepared two bedrooms with her best linen and sent to the village for Mrs. Pleasance Nudds, who helps her.

While locals dropped in to the bar for a pint, a game of darts and a sing song, Gwen served the princes with hot vegetable soup followed by roast beef and Yorkshire pudding in the cream and pink dining-room.

Later, the Prince of Wales watched television in the tiny lounge. When it was

"time, gentlemen, please," Gwen and her husband, Alfred, completed all their nightly chores and followed the princes upstairs to bed.

Early next morning Gwen served her royal guests with eggs, bacon and toast.

Duke or dustman, royalty or commoner, anyone can find peace from the bustling world here at Hickling.

For less than ten pounds a week you can eat from the little oak table the princes used, or sleep in the beds the princes slept in.

That is, if you are prepared to sleep in each of the six single beds in each of the three bedrooms in turn. Because no one will tell you exactly which was which.

Gwen Amis is keeping that secret to herself.

Tom Grapes

Boat Builder

Tom was born in Fleggburgh. His parents moved to Ludham when he was very young, and he has continued to live there for the past sixty-five years. One of his more vivid childhood memories, apart from the daily pleasures of freedom to roam river and marsh, was a summer fishing trip with some boyhood friends. A violent storm forced the boys to shelter in the ruins of St Benet's Abbey. Under some sacks Tom discovered a transmitter. They told the local police of their find and subsequently two Germans were picked up in Wroxham. However the boys learnt nothing further from their find.

When Tom left the local school, he found employment working in private gardens. Next he joined the marines. After the war he applied to the Ludham Boat Yard, prepared to do any job. On the same day he also joined the local fire brigade. As volunteers, they won the Norfolk area competition against paid firemen. Their record of completing the fire hydrant drill in forty-seven seconds stood for a long time, and Tom was one of that four-man team. Besides winning the shield, the men were given national savings stamps. In 1947 Tom's wages at the boat yard were £4 to £5 weekly. He received only twenty-eight shillings weekly whilst serving in the marines and £1 weekly as a gardener. Tom well remembers the long hard winter of 1947/8. In the unheated boat-shed he was given the rough jobs, scraping down and varnishing old dinghies. Within three years his wages had risen to £7 a week and his skills in boat-building were developing fast.

The Hunters' Yard at Ludham was run by a father, his two sons and two labourers. Mr Percy Hunter began his career in the boat business as manager of the Norfolk Broads Yacht Company, Wroxham, later he transferred as manager to Applegates Boat Yard, Potter Heigham. In 1931, Mr Hunter bought land from a friendly farmer, and a boat-shed and a dyke were constructed.

Percy Hunter

16

Mr Percy Hunter, and his two sons Cyril and Stanley, started building boats in 1932; two were built annually until the second world war halted these activities. In 1932, *Lustre* and *Lullaby* were built, and the following year *Luna* and *Wood Sorrel* were completed. Son Cyril was the boat builder whilst Stanley did the varnishing. During the war the boat yard was closed and Mr Hunter went to Herbert Woods to help build air-sea rescue craft and landing craft. Cyril and Stanley were drafted to Thorneycroft to help with the war efforts, building boats for the armed forces.

Tom worked for the Hunters' family business from 1947 to 1968 when the yard was bought by the Norfolk Council and from here the County's Sailing Base still operates. Tom retired from the Base in 1994 after forty-nine years' service; however, after three weeks' holiday, he was asked to return to help 'rig out'

Tom Grapes rigging
Wood Anemone

the fleet and get them ready for the hiring season. Each Saturday and Monday Tom still continues to work at the yard.

This unique fleet of engineless yachts were all of carvel construction. In Tom's first apprenticed year he helped to build *Wood Anemone*. His job consisted of holding on to the copper nails as they were clinched. *Wood Avens* was built two years later, and by then Tom's contribution to its building was a great deal more involved. With carvel-built boats the frames were built first and the strakes fastened to them; the strakes do not overlap as in clinker construction, instead they are butted together edge to edge.

Tom remembers wherries visiting the yard. In the early days there was no quay heading in the dyke. Many yachts had 10 - 14 foot bowsprits and they merely ran into the reeds. Two memorable Broadland wherry skippers visiting the yard were Bob Bates in *Olive* and Barney Matthews in *Reed Bird*. Tom's eyes twinkled as he recalled one old skipper of over seventy years. 'Half his teeth were missing, and he cooked the meat so tough that a fork wouldn't go in the gravy'.

17

Midway through this century, sailing yachts out-numbered motor boats by ten to one, and huge fleets of yachts were available for hire. Gradually yachts were sold off or broken up to make way for the growing number of motor boats. The entire fleet of Shearwater yachts built by Hunters was broken up, 'There was nothing wrong with them', commented Tom. He also spoke with regret of the breaking up of *Sunbeam*. 'She had lovely lines', was his sad comment. As the years went by, many of the yards were taken over or ceased trading. Chumney & Hawk alone had forty hire yachts. Jack Powles had a thriving business and Collins owned the wherry yacht*s Olive*, *White Moth* and *Norada*. Herbert Woods Ltd., one of the biggest boat building firms, established in 1920, had a hire fleet of forty-three motor cruisers and twenty yachts by 1934. 'Too many changes', said Tom, 'But the hirers don't change. Sailors are always the same'. Asked for a story of past hirers, Tom volunteered the following: A well-known bank had an annual hiring for many years. The first night of one particular year, the men celebrated in the local pub. During the night one of the crew came up on deck to answer a call of nature and found that the wind had changed direction. He therefore re-moored the boat, pointing it in the opposite direction. When the next man came up on deck to have a pee, instead of stepping on to the bank, he stepped into the river. 'That sobered him up', was the dry comment from Tom.

Originally Taylors of Wroxham supplied the wood needed for Hunters' Yard. A complete tree would be bought and cut up. Even today, the same system for seasoning the wood continues. Splints of wood are still inserted between the widths, allowing air to circulate. In 1938, Percy Hunter found some high quality Honduras mahogany in Taylor's yard, but it was planed for railway carriages. However it ended up in *Woodcut 2*. The widths cut from the tree fitted flush and the joints were so tight that no caulking was necessary. Three craftsmen continue to restore and maintain the Hunter fleet continuing the same methods used in the early days. 'Nothing can replace work done by hand and eye', said Tom, 'but there are more electric saws and planers to help these days'.

The original steamers are still used. 'All hands on deck' is the call when a rib is rushed out of the steamer, and all the men in the yard have to be quick to cramp the wood into position. 'If the wood cools off before this is done, it will break', explained Tom. At present, the yard has difficulty in finding satisfactory wood for masts and quants. The best supply used to come from Norway and it was brought over as deck cargo. Being cold grown the annual rings were close together. Poles from a Welsh firm were tried, but the annual rings were ½" apart and proved useless for quant production. Tom showed me some painted lettering on the transom of a yacht. Some years ago the B.B.C. rented *Lullaby* for several weeks to reconstruct and film Arthur Ransome's book *Coot Club* and the *Big Six*. *Teasel* was painted on *Lullaby's* transom to convert her for the filming. 'Who did the lettering?', I asked. 'Just picked it up', replied Tom. Next I was shown some beautiful wood blocks that had been made in the yard. Caressing them, Tom handled them like works of art, which they are.

Lullaby **becomes** *Teasel* **for the television film of Arthur Ransome's books**

No new boats are now built at the yard; however restoration and repair keeps three men busy all year round. 'The fleets get hard hiring', said Tom. 'The topsides of the yachts have been replanked, but the bottoms are the originals.' I learnt that there were no lets after the first week in October. The boats are brought in, scrubbed out and de-rigged. Pulling out takes one to two days; nine yachts go in the first shed whilst the remaining four and the half-deckers are stored in the second shed.

Rubbing down to get the old wood back with a nice colour, then re-varnishing, is a winter job. If Easter falls early, there may still be a skin of ice in the dyke and the new varnish may be cut to pieces by the early hirers. Tom pointed out a spare mast wrapped in canvas stored in the rafters of a shed and several quants leaning beside it. 'A hirer loses very little holiday time', explained Tom. A broken mast can be substituted and another quant supplied very quickly.

Preparing to leave the yard, Tom said, 'You can't go without a sail'. Protesting, (but without any conviction) that I had already taken up too much of his time on his day off, I was enchanted to help roll back the cover from *Wood Avens*. With years of long experience, Tom rigged the sails and quanted out of the dyke. It was a perfect June day. Broadland was in her most beguiling mood; blue sky, fluffy white clouds, shafts of sun lingering over the swaying reed beds and marshes and a good breeze that showed off the yacht's superb handling. Sailing along the metallic blue river, Tom recalled the past. 'You would find white water lilies in every little bay along the Thurne', he said. 'Nowadays the water is churned up continuously and the mud doesn't get a chance to settle'. A great white plastic motor cruiser overtook us and roared past in a flurry of frothy wash as if to emphasise this point. Low land around the marshes used to absorb the overflow at high tides, but nowadays the farmers crop the marshes and wonder why the winter wheat is regularly lost due to flooding. 'The original centuries-long custom of keeping the marshes at different levels and pumping water off them into the drains and dykes proved satisfactory', said Tom. He thought the present idea of the Yare barrier was too artificial and would prove too costly. 'The farmers only are in favour of it', he commented. 'It would give them more land for agriculture'.

Two hours later, replacing the cover on *Wood Avens*, I asked Tom, after nearly half a century spent looking after this unique fleet of mahogany and redwood cruisers, did retirement come hard. 'I have many hobbies', he replied, 'I love all sports and I especially enjoy shooting; anyhow, after three weeks' holiday when I retired in November 1994, I returned to help with the hire fleet two days a week. I mainly do the rigging now. In the old days, all the sails were Egyptian cotton and the ropes were manilla or hemp, and in the winter you had to break the ice in the varnish pot, so I won't miss that part of the job'.

Leaving a magic corner of Broadland, where that boat shed cloisters so many memories, I saw that the marsh that originally housed Percy Hunter and Sons' Yard, which in 1968 was bought by the Norfolk County Council as its sailing base, now also houses the Broads Authority Field Base and Wherry Trust offices.

That evening, I read the old boat catalogue that Tom lent to me. Hire price comparisons were interesting. *Lullaby, Lustre* and *Luna* could be rented out for about £35 per week, with the *Hustler* class boats costing between £19 and £22 for the weekly hire in the nineteen-seventies. By the nineteen-nineties, the *Lullabys* four-berth yachts cost £388 per week in high season, with the *Hustler* class two-berth yachts costing £ 275.

In another book that Tom lent me, the *Norfolk Broads Holiday Book 1935*, I learnt that the Auxiliary Wherry Yacht *Olive* could be hired for £26.10 weekly in high season as could *Norada*. Both these wherry yachts had the services of two attendants and a portable bath. Electric light was optional on many yachts in the hire fleets, and cost 7/6d per week extra if required. Both these wherries sail regularly round Broadland to this day, a magnificent sight.

Early in 1995, the Norfolk County Council decided to sell off the fleet of boats at their Ludham Base. Dr George Turner, Education County Committee Chairman, said, 'We would prefer not to sell, but faced with the cuts we're facing, it's an asset and we need the money'. However, there was such a national outcry condemning this proposed sale, that instead, the Heritage Yacht Fleet Fund has been set up, and hopefully this unique, motorless, wooden boat fleet built at Hunter's Yard will stay on in Norfolk intact. The modern plastic yacht, hired out with every known comfort, from T.V. set to fridge/freezer, video recorder and washing machine, cannot give greater pleasure to the hirer than the Hunter boats.

Richard Starling

Hon. Warden of Martham and West Somerton

Richard Starling met me one cold grey day in November. It was at the suggestion of Christopher Cadbury that I went to see him. I soon found out why he was held in such esteem by that world-travelled conservationist. Richard had piercing blue eyes and a swarthy face such as one would expect from somebody who is warden of a well-cared-for Nature Reserve, spending most of his days outside, around Martham and West Somerton.

As we walked towards the mill, Richard's eyes were constantly probing for information on the ground and in the sky. Soft-spoken, and with a trace of Norfolk dialect, he told me that he had gone to school at West Somerton. 'With only 30 pupils in the school, we enjoyed a lot of individual attention,' he remarked. After a spell in the Merchant Navy, Richard returned to Norfolk. 'I never really left,' he commented.

In 1971 Martham Broad was bought by Mr Cadbury and given to the Norfolk Naturalists Trust. 'This Nature reserve is the most important of all Broadland sites as it is one of the very few that still has clear water,' I read in the excellent leaflet produced by the Trust. The leaflet went on to explain: 'Unlike other broads, Martham has not been isolated from the river system, but is still connected to the river Thurne. However the upper reaches of this river where Martham is sited, are not affected by sewage effluent, and therefore the water entering the broad is relatively pure.' In 1983 Frank Pigg retired. He asked Richard Starling to continue his work on the marshes.

By now we had walked through the well kept village and along the footpath on the north side of the Parish Staithe boat dyke. 'The last wherry using this staithe loaded sugar beet - and I still use it to off-load the reed and sedge harvest,' commented Richard. 'The owners of the adjoining boat dyke, the local drainage board, could fill these moorings with private boats, but I'm sure this would be very unpopular with the villagers, the holiday-makers who use the moorings as well as with the landlord of the Lion public house. The moorings are kept empty during the winter months when peace returns to the area after the hire-craft season finishes. I confess that I enjoy the winter months with few boats on the river'.

As we approached Martham mill, Richard paused to read the water-

Sedge Harvesting Richard Starling on the right

level, which he did daily. 'Fourteen inches above datum - haven't gone metric yet' he said with a twinkle. 'It's about right for this time of the year.' He pointed out the clear water, and plentiful supply of weed, especially Canadian pondweed and star-wort floating in crystal clear water with the bottom easily seen. Richard showed me the rare holly-leaved naiad. 'We've always had it in the broad, but this year we found it in the river where the holiday craft moor,' he said with justifiable pride.

I remembered then one of my favourite sails on the Northern rivers was to launch at Hickling, sail across the Broad and along Heigham Sound towards the upper Thurne. If the swing bridge at Martham Ferry was open, it was easy to sail on, but often the ferry was closed, and with the boatyard's hire fleet congesting the narrow river I often had a lively time. However, a mile further on was the most idyllic, peaceful narrow waterway. I would always pause and leave Wanderbug's hull in the middle of the waterway, her bows over the clear water and her stern over the muddy opaque water, and just enjoy looking. During the summer, large yellow and white waterlilies lined the riverbank, and on the banks ragged robin, purple and yellow loosestrife, marsh orchids and sow thistle grew in profusion. Frequently I was rewarded by close views of the glorious swallowtail butterfly, and knew that the large milk parsley plants, which feed the caterpillar of the species, was responsible for the survival of this rare butterfly in Broadland. As I sailed on, passing glimpses of Martham Broads to the left and right of the river through the reed beds, I had always been tempted to row into the broad to see why it felt so different from all the other places I sailed past..... Today, meeting Richard Starling gave me some of the answers.

'Caught anything?' asked a friendly Richard as we passed two fishermen seated on the banks of the river. 'We rely on them to keep us informed. Generally, fisherman are anxious to preserve wildlife, and keep the environment healthy. Good catches of rudd and perch indicate that the water quality is satisfactory,' he explained as we reached Martham mill. The sails had blown down in 1953, but the brick walls were in a good state of repair. Tools leaned against the inner white-washed walls of the ground floor of the mill. There was a long-handled scythe, a meg and a crome. Richard makes his own handles for his tools. Oars were there too. Outside in the dyke lay an open boat painted dark green. Richard told me he had designed it on the lines of a lighter. It is built locally and used by Richard on the reserve for a variety of tasks.

We climbed into the upper room of the mill, and sitting on a bench below the window, Richard passed me his binoculars. I caught my breath. The view was staggeringly beautiful and one that I shall never forget. Shafts of sun shot through grey clouds. Seaward were Winterton sand-dunes, and before us were the two broads. The whole reserve consists of 60 hectares, with reed and sedge beds, scrub and woodland surrounding the broads. The honorary warden checked the two boats on the north broad. He also checked that a passing hire cruiser kept to the correct channel. 'Birds are not disturbed here, as holiday craft are not allowed in either broad' explained Richard, and he listed the winter bird population of wigeon, teal, pochard and gadwall. Hen harriers hunted over the reed beds as did marsh harriers; bearded tits and warblers used the reed and sedge beds, whilst common terns rested on platforms moored in the broads.

Richard pointed out the blocks of cut reed and sedge. The golden squares of colour were clearly seen from our aerial view. Scrapes and water, cleared so that waders could feed and rest, were also highlighted on the patchwork beneath us. 'I cut the sedge in blocks on a four-year rotation, whilst the reed beds are cut every two years,' said Richard. I could see the well-maintained network of dykes winding between his harvesting. All the sedge and reed is carried out of the marshes by boat. 'It is difficult to keep this area private. Everybody has the same right to enjoy wildlife. We have known big pike here and roach; bream and perch do well, but it is so difficult to control people.' He handed me the application for a fishing permit which he had helped the Trust prepare. No less than twenty-one guidelines and rules were drawn up for people wishing to day-fish on Martham Broad.

No motor boats, radios, mud weights or boats with masts were to be taken on to the broad. Fishing was limited to two boats at a time, and designated positions had to be used by them. Only two permit holders, each using a maximum of two rods, were to be allowed in each boat. Each of these small open boats accepted on to the broad had to fish only between the hours of 08.00 and 16.00 hours. The days for fishing were Thursdays, Fridays and Saturdays between the months of October and March. The last guideline printed on the sheet showed an endearing care for the fish: 'In the interest of the welfare of fish, anglers must have a soft material layer, e.g. piece of carpeting, covering the inside floorboards where fish are to be placed during handling.' How I wished that these guidelines could be accepted by all Broadland fishermen. On a cold January sail recently, Hickling was grey, wild and very beautiful, yet I was saddened to see young men in boats fishing with their boats pulled into the reed beds and using several rods - and swearing at us, in one lonely sailing boat, for disturbing their fishing.

'We've got to go back and look at these places when they were successful. We must persuade people to respect these areas and to realise that the wldlife comes first, which is the reason for the site being a National Nature Reserve. Fortunately, most people do respect the area, but a small minority often cause problems with litter, noise and disturbance,' Richard said. He admitted, however, 'We are lucky here - sometimes I go round and visit other reserves and realise how fortunate we are in Norfolk.' Whilst modern marketing of the Broads and tourism doesn't help the well-being of some sections of wild life, Richard told me the Broads Authority had helped set up an apprenticeship scheme for a reed-cutter to work with him on the reserve; 'they send in gangs of helpers to clear scrub and clean up the area and more recently have improved the site for bitterns and other rare birds,' enlarged Richard.

Being a self-employed marshman and honorary warden, Richard has little time for committees. He talked about 'a veil of silence' and said with a wry smile, 'Office staff seem to come and go and some appear more interested in their own careers than actually having any impact on the reserves. The gap between management and those doing the work has sadly widened.'

Richard Starling's philosophy of seeking a stronger partnership between the Trust and their workmen, and of creating good management of the marshes so that food and nesting sites will entice the wading birds to return to breed, was a subject he kept returning to. 'If the bittern left, that would be a terrible failure. We have two pairs of resident birds in the area, and the continental bittern over-winter on our marshes. We keep the anglers away from the bays where over-wintering birds feed and some of our rarer birds nest, and in the upper Thurne there aren't so many banks which fishermen can use, so they have to fish from boats. We have hawks, owls, snipe, reed warblers and sedge warblers all using Martham Broad. If the management is right, the bird population should remain constant.'

With my eyes glued to the wonderful panoramic view beneath me and unwilling to leave the mill, I asked Richard how he organised his day, and what was his workload. He told me that his busy time started in December when he began reed-cutting. Harvesting of the sedge and reed harvest, which he sells to thatchers, is his main source of income. This last year 1993/4 there was a decline in the quality of the reed beds; the water was high and stayed on the beds too long and didn't flow. Richard also patrolled the reserve at different times of the day and night, also relying on the fishermen to be aware of happenings in the reserve. Repairs to the boathouse ('We had a kingfisher, kestrels and owls in there this year') and mill and general management of the marshes kept him busy. He spoke without bitterness of 'banking-style conservation, of 09.00 hrs to 18.00 hours, and closed at weekends... Wildlife lives seven days a week, we work those hours too, it is only the Conservation offices that keep a five day week.'

Richard spoke of his concern for a strong Broadland; he saw its deterioration continuing unless a strong policy was adopted. 'Too much money is spent on salaries in offices, and on administration,' he said, the marshmen and field workers needed more support. 'Do you feel isolated?' I asked. 'I like the freedom and the isolation,' he replied 'but I could do with more back-up'. He told me of a visit to a Dutch National Park similar to the Broads area. 'There were three people in the office and forty-two others out reed-cutting when I was there. They control the water-levels effectively so that they can go on working. It was a wonderful experience to see their back-up. There was no division between the labour force; the head man could cut reed as well as the next. We don't need research as much as men out there on the marshes doing management the way it was

Richard Starling ferrying Christopher Cadbury and his guests from Whiteslea

always done. Sadly, here the balance is tipped heavily the other way, and like an inverted pyramid it's bound to collapse when people ask where all the money is spent.'

As we locked up the mill and walked back through the village, Richard Starling spoke again of Christopher Cadbury. 'He has great vision; he is always thinking two years ahead. He is so easy to work with. He is very demanding because he has vision - but he will listen to your problems. He has been very good to us.'

Mr Starling took me home to have some hot tea. Walking through the garden I asked about some bundles of reed lying there. 'That's Polish reed,' he explained, 'I wanted to see the difference.' Pointing to a house opposite he said proudly 'That is my reed and that is my sedge on the ridge.'

Richard's father is a farmer, his brothers are agricultural workers, whilst he, a self-employed reed-cutter and marshman, in his own words is 'one of a dying breed.' Despite his concern for the future of Broadland, in that happy home, with wood-burner keeping out the dull November gloom, there was also enormous wisdom and awareness and pride in the reserve. This was being passed on to his son Robert who told me that he wanted to do what his father did when he grew up. He also said he would like a gun 'to control people'! So another independent, caring, knowledgeable warden may well follow in Richard Starling's footsteps in the years ahead. Martham Broads certainly are a success story!

27

Ted and Phyllis Ellis

Naturalists

Ted Ellis was born in Guernsey in 1909 of Norfolk parents. He will always be remembered as one of Norfolk's best-known naturalists, broadcasters and writers. From 1928-1956 he was Keeper of Natural History at the Castle Museum in Norwich. Living for 40 years with his wife Phyllis and their five children at Wheatfen, Surlingham, an isolated brick and wood house converted from a pair of marshman's cottages, Ted's enthusiasm for researching and recording the flora and fauna surrounding Wheatfen was unique. His radio and television programme became so popular that in the 1980's Ted's regular audience was estimated at half a million - a record-breaking figure for BBC Norfolk at that time. As well as beautiful photographic slides (he built up a library of 18,000) Ted would also take living specimens into the studios, often staggering beneath boxes of grasses, reeds and jam jars full of specimens - nothing was forgotten for his broadcasts, except once when he forgot his own false teeth!

In 1982 Ted Ellis was awarded the Royal Television Society's regional award for his contribution to television. His weekly radio programme, 'Nature Postbag', was equally popular. Ted left school at fifteen without having taken any exams. However in 1970 he was awarded an honorary doctorate by the University of East Anglia. As a communicator and as a naturalist he was in great demand as a speaker. His enthusiasm knew no bounds, and in one year alone he had to turn down over 200 requests to speak - that was in addition to carrying out several evening lectures weekly, filling the University's lecture theatre one night and the next having standing-room only in a local village hall. At one such evening, at a Women's Institute meeting, he found the Queen Mother and the Queen as part of his audience.

Until two days before his death, Ted was still writing natural history articles for the Eastern Daily Press. He had written a daily nature article in this local paper for nearly 40 years and also a fortnightly one in the *Guardian* newspaper over a period of 17 years. His best known work, *The Broads - a Natural History of Broadland*, was published by Collins in the 'New Naturalist' series in 1965. He died in July 1986 and shortly after his death the Norfolk Naturalists Trust and the Norwich Naturalists Society jointly awarded the Sydney Long Memorial Medal posthumously to commemorate his 'unique knowledge of natural history in Norfolk.'

Characteristically Ted Ellis, who was nationally known as a conservationist long before environmental matters were as popular as they are today, asked for a simple funeral. The village church at Surlingham hosted the celebration of his life and was decorated with wild flowers. Phyllis played the church organ as she had done every Sunday for many years, and she was accompanied by several of the family playing a mixture of instruments. At the graveside, recorders and violins played medieval music... Nearly ten years on, I came unexpectedly upon Ted's grave. I had been spending the day with *Wanderbug* sailing along the River Yare. The wind had died, the tide was foul, so I tied my dinghy to a bank side and got out to stretch my legs. The riverside track took me up a little hill where the ruins of a church, St Saviour's, was situated. Walking towards it I saw the gravestone of Ted Ellis, the first grave dug there since the eighteenth century. I sat on the grassy slope and thought of Ted's life. The Yare Valley, following a broad curve of marsh which is a bird sanctuary, made it a most peaceful spot to give thanks and remember a great naturalist. Later, on that same walk, I stopped to enter the bird hides built overlooking the marshes. The second one was a memorial to Ted Ellis.

It is said that behind every great man is a strong woman. Phyllis Ellis certainly fulfils this role. Ted and Phyllis Ellis married in 1938. They lived in Norwich. Phyllis recalled they had a small house and quarter of an acre of garden with a front lawn which they sowed with crimson clover much to their neighbours' amazement. With bombing and air raids a regular event in their young married lives, it must have been a grim time. After living on in their

Wedding Day

29

bomb-ravaged house, it was finally razed to the ground in a raid in 1942. They lost all their family possessions, yet Ted was seen to rescue a jam jar of water beetles while volunteers fought to quench the flames around his home.

In 1945 the Ellis's second child was born and the family was offered the lease of two damp eighteenth-century marshmen's cottages, with 150 acres of fen, seven miles outside Norwich. Two young children, one a baby, in a home that was very dilapidated, no electricity or gas, water to be drawn from a well, and half a mile from the village of Surlingham, with the tide lapping the side of the house would have defeated many young couples, yet Phyllis said 'It was our idea of heaven.' She dried nappies in front of an open fire from branches that she had dragged out of the woods and chopped up single-handed.

Ted, working in Norwich, saw little of his home in those early days, travelling into the Castle Museum before the rush hour and returning near dusk. Wheatfen soon had a vegetable garden and, as Ted's fame as writer and radio personality spread, Phyllis had to cope with large numbers of visitors as well as being mother of a young family. One such visit was remembered especially: in 1948 a party from a Scientific Society came to enjoy the fen marshes. Leaving the boat, they had to trudge through the wet, boggy path in a violent summer storm. All fifty of them were given hot tea and scones as they dried out in the house.

As Ted continued to catalogue the wild life at Wheatfen, his wife also had elderly people to care for at home, Ted's mother and Phyllis's father and uncle. One day she said 'I don't know what I'd do if we had a fire - because we have paraffin lamps and candles all over the house! Who should I rescue first? Should I get out the baby and children or the old people?'

Ted's health, which had never been strong, deteriorated. He was off work for over a year. So in 1951 Phyllis decided to return to full-time work. She had trained as an elementary teacher at Goldsmith's College in 1931 specialising in Maths and music, and with four children and a husband to support, her temporary teaching work became full time. 'I was very strict,' she confided 'but I loved the work.'

In the early 1950s groups of young undergraduate students came to do research and camp in the woods. Eventually eight universities took part in annual projects at Wheatfen. In 1953 Ted and Phyllis had their fifth child and the happy family nurtured music-making in the home. The children learnt to harmonise as they sang together over the washing up and at summer barbecues in the woods. The Ellis's were natural home-makers and organisers and Wheatfen was open house to scientific people and friends from all over the world. Presiding over such meetings, Phyllis, practical and full of generosity, could be heard calling from the kitchen to the scientific gathering, 'Come on Dr Whats-your-name, have another sausage.'

Hospitality at Wheatfen extended to all living things and, as the children brought home injured animals and birds, a hospital was set up for owls, a bittern, a one-legged heron, field mice and bats. It is reported that Phyllis refused to house gulls.

She cycled three miles to teach until she retired, nursed and hassled her husband to meet deadlines in his winter work, and tried to protect him from over-exploitation. He never used an agent. In 1985, when he was terminally ill, Ted is reported to have said, 'I wouldn't like Wheatfen to go to someone who would spoil it by `gardening'. I hope it will go to someone who will look after it by not looking after it, as I have done.'

Night Noises, Surlingham - April 1st 1974
From one of Ted's contributions to the *Eastern Daily Press*

Even at night one can feel something of the magic of spring just now. When the sky remains clear after sundown there is soon a chill in the air but this seems to distil the fragrances of the mossy earth, grass, pine needles, sallow bloom and various tender herbs in the hedgerows as night mists gather.

Recently I took a walk in starlight with a tip-tilted half moon hanging in the western sky. A field pond was steaming like a witches' cauldron as mist was generated from its vapours. There was enough light in the sky to throw black snaking shadows on trees across the road, and I could even see wayside gorse blossoms looking as pale as the moon itself. There was perfect calm, with long periods of absolute silence, in this Broadland valley, but if one listened carefully, small night noises could be detected from time to time, such as the brief utterances of wild ducks, and moorhens on the waterways, and the mooing of coypu in the swamps, and the caterwauling of owls. At one point I was momentarily startled by a wood mouse leaping and racing over the road, and I am sure I heard a hedgehog snuffling in the undergrowth...

31

I only met Ted Ellis once. I was one of the thousands of students that he enthused about his specialist subject - fungi - and it was eight years after Phyllis had been widowed that I met her. *Wanderbug* and I had joined the friendly Coldham Hall Sailing Club a year or two prior to that meeting, and John, her son, then commodore of the S.C., had helped me extend my sailing time on the Yare. So the Ellis hospitality was being carried on.

Phoning Phyllis to arrange to see her after one such sailing day, I was told: 'Ring me before 8.00 am to check that I'll be in.' I was to find out that this remarkably enthusiastic octogenarian still had the boundless energy of ladies half her age. Her regular talks on Radio Norfolk showed her to be passionate about environmental issues as wide-ranging as the proposal to sell off Thetford Forest to the Yare Valley Barrier. I had heard her several times on the radio and was expecting to meet a large bombastic woman; instead a tall graceful feminine lady answered the door to Wheatfen. 'You are lucky to find me in' she said, ushering me into a cosy kitchen which looked out on to the wilderness garden. 'I go down to the fen to do the tides daily and there is always the garden to tackle.'

We walked through the house. Having been bombed twice, much of the family furniture had gone, but a large piano, comfortable open fireplace, paper-piled bureau (bought in a sale at Acle), sink-in armchairs, floor rugs which were thrown over wooden floors, and three large embroidered pictures, sewn by Alice, Ted's mother, hung on the cream emulsioned walls of the living room and created an air of comfort and peace. There was a comforting smell of wax polish pervading the room. 'I used to make my own' Phyllis said with a smile. In the kitchen were stacked up books, boxes of slides, and photographs on the walls. Ted's influence and interests were alive everywhere. The walk-in practical pantry led off the small kitchen and I was not surprised to see a double sink and a wood-burning Rayburn. I expressed interest however that Phyllis should invest in something as modern and materialistic as a microwave oven. 'Oh my dear, when you come off the marshes and the garden, you want hot food quickly,' said this practical grandmother.

Many widows live in the past as they are left to live on alone. Phyllis's energy has come out of the shadows of her famous husband to create an enthusiasm and practical life which ensures that the Ted Ellis Trust continues and expands his work at Wheatfen. The Trust has bought one hundred acres of reed bed, tidal channel and carr which still contains such a wide diversity of plants and animals and it aims to keep this broad and its wildlife accessible for the enjoyment and education of children, students and adults. Two attractive wooden buildings and a large sympathetically-planned car park, a walkway to allow wheelchair-bound people to have access to this wildlife wilderness have been planned since Ted's death. Phyllis's energy is directed in many ways to create money on which the Trust expands. Her diary rarely has a free day in it. 'I hate giving talks during the summer,' she told me, as we walked round her vegetable beds at the back of the house, but she does talks and slide shows to many organisations, from village Women's Institutes to Townswomen's Guilds, and organises coffee mornings, jumble sales and wine and cheese evenings. 'I don't have an original idea in my head,' she admitted cheerfully 'but I pick up other people's ideas, and I can campaign. I love to help the handicapped and I enjoy showing Ted's slides to groups of people. It's all publicity for the Trust. Art exhibitions, concerts, and plant stalls in the garden are other aspects of her money-raising activities. Her aim is to make as many Friends of the Ted Ellis Trust as possible. 'We should reach six hundred soon.'

So Ted's Wheatfen reserve which consists of reed beds, open fen, sallow-scrub, and small broads is being cared for as Ted would have wished, and visitors may see southern marsh orchids, opposite-leaved golden saxifrage, foxgloves, ragged robbin, milk parsley, willow herb and nettles, hemp agrimony and adders tongue fern, and they may walk beside peat diggings, through wet woodland and along reed beds. A wide variety of birds and animals thrive in this fen. A warden is anxious to share, helpful and enthusiastic about his work. Dr David Bellamy is reported to have said 'Wheatfen Broad is, in its own way, as important as Mount Everest or the giant redwood forests of North America. It is probably the best bit of fenland we have, because we know so much about it. That is purely because one man gave his life to trying to understand it . . .'

Phyllis has allowed the Trust to extend a nature trail into Surlingham Wood and the Carr, so the increased paths now cover over three miles for visitors to enjoy. Due to the improved water quality in the reserve, star-wort has returned to the 130 acre site, after disappearing for many years. Dredging the dykes, clearing willows, creating better conditions for the reed beds to flourish (because reed beds purify the water) is work that has enabled this fragile fen to flourish.

In 1994 the Trust was presented with a cash prize of over one thousand pounds to commemorate five years work by the Ted Ellis Trust. 'It will pay the fees of people working in the Fen for a short time,' said a modest Phyllis, practical as ever. Now in the school room in the Ted Ellis Trust's centre there is a plaque recognising the work of the Trust. The plaque was the final touch to Anglian Water's 'Caring for the Environment' prize.

The second time I walked down the country lane to visit Phyllis at Wheatfen it was a grey day. I enjoyed the golden flashes of sun splashing across the field lining the muddy lane. Rhododendron bushes, silver birch trees, green-yellow oaks, ferns and brambles lined the path to the cottage, I heard laughter in the garden and saw that there was a group of handicapped children visiting the reserve. A smiling Phyllis hosted the party. Later, when I apologised for interrupting her, she said 'You are welcome, but I'm tired. I'm always up at six but this group rang up and I couldn't put them off.' 'You must come and have a sail with me soon,' I invited, as a way of thanking her. 'Oh I'd love that' she replied. 'My parents had boats, and I taught my children to sail on Rockland Broad.' Phyllis who says she 'avoids housework' and prefers to live most of her days outside then began to prepare for an evening lecture - her third that week.

Ted Ellis at Surlingham

Bob Mace

Marshman

Luckily I was early for my appointment with Bob. We were to meet at the Norwich Cattle Market at noon. When I telephoned him earlier at his home to ask if we could talk about his life on the marshes, his cheerful acceptance was: 'Oun't do any harm'. I laughed, 'You can tell me to push off if you don't like my questions'. 'I'll soon do that,' he replied.

It was a raw day in late January when we first met, but Bob wore only an open-necked shirt under his jacket. His ruddy cheerful face looked years younger than his sixty years. I found out quickly that Bob was no respecter of persons. A Broads Authority employee kept him waiting - twice - having telephoned him to arrange a meeting on the marshes. The first time Bob waited half an hour, the second time he left after five minutes, later telling a university lecturer who had trained the young lady, 'You oughter teach her some bloody manners'.

Bob and his wife have lived on Haddiscoe Island for 38 years. They moved into a bungalow by the marshes in 1956. There is no made-up road to the bungalow, and the nearest road is 4 miles away. Their only son went to school, two miles from home, by boat, and Bob's father-in-law made the journey to Reedham with the small boy. 'Are you lonely?' I asked. 'It's a very good life,' replied Bob. 'What about your wife?' I enquired. 'She can't drive, so she can only go out when I take her, which is to do the shopping once a week.' Bob commented cheerfully that they last had a holiday in 1977, and that was the first one for 25 years. 'Can't get away in the summer because of the cattle, and in the winter you daren't leave the house for fear of flooding'.

Bob told me that he was self-employed, being paid by the marsh owners who were the Askew Trust. The Haddiscoe marshes covered 2,000 acres and three men worked on them. Bob's level was 700 acres. His son also worked on the marshes and lived next door to his own bungalow. On Haddiscoe island are four houses and two windmills, one of which is a holiday home owned by people living in Kent. The other one is being carefully restored by a Londoner and his wife. There used to be four mills: Six Mile Mill, which had cloth sails and was turned by hand, Toft

35

Monks Mill, Pettingill Mill, and Five Mile Mill.

Bob's winter work was to 'draw' dykes. The work involved cleaning 13 miles of dykes. He also had 18 miles of drains to keep clear of weeds and mud. His tools for this seasonal work from September to Easter were a meg, a dydle, a cutter and a chrome. A shuff, a wooden tool with a scythe riveted to its side, took out the mud. 'It was all knee and wrist work,' explained Bob. In 1956 Bob's weekly wage was about £5. It was piece-work and the wage was 10 shillings and sixpence a score for dykes (a 'score' was 5 chains in length). In a good day a man could clear 2 score - but only 1½ score if the dykes were full of weed. Cleaning drains was an easier way to earn good money. A man could cope with 4 score daily.

Bob Mace with his cattle on the marshes

The winter work in the 1990s has changed little over the last thirty years. Summer times the marshes are used for grazing animals. The work involves a seven day week. The cattle have to be counted daily on Bob's 700 acres. He is responsible for 900 cattle and 2,000 sheep. 'We do all the basic veterinary work like worming,' said Bob 'and we pull the animals out of the dykes'. Bob's summer wages are paid by the farmers who rent the marshes. 'They are good marshes,' said Bob with pride. 'The cattle put on 2½ cwt per annum. Some customers have been coming to us for over 30 years. The marshes are let out for the summer grazing to the highest bidders, and farmers from Cromer, Diss and as far away as Essex use them.' I was told that the letting season was from April 1st to September 31st. 'I give a whistle and they come to me,' said Bob, referring to his cattle with affection. He was less enthusiastic about the sheep. 'I hate them' he said with a twinkle in his eyes . 'I've got no affinity with them. They don't have a will to live. Don't give you any encouragement to look arter them. Some die for the sake of dying. We're always running about with dead sheep!'

Bob and I talked next about Norfolk's countryside plans for the future. On his marshes, reed-cutting was declining due to pollution from boats and the saline waters washing over the reed beds or ronds from the river Waveney, he thought. 'We used to get 15-18 thousand bunches up to 2 years ago, except the drought year of 1976. Now we only cut about 800 bundles annually. Pollution must play a big part in this, because years ago when we burnt the reeds we got white smoke, and now it is black!'

The day I first met Bob was the 40th anniversary of the East Anglian floods. He told me how he worked during 1953 for 7 weeks to clear the flood water before the fresh water returned. 'There were two of us and we worked in 4-hour shifts pumping, using a tractor and an admiralty pump lent by the government,' recalled Bob. 'We lived in Six Mile house windmill. We nailed sacks around the walls to keep out the draught and there was an old grate in which we burned scrap wood to keep warm. We only went home to get fresh grub. We used 14,000 gallons of petrol running the tractor; it used 4 gallons every hour'.

I asked Bob about the 1993 proposed barriers to protect Broadland from flooding. A barrier across the Bure, or one on the river Yare have been talked about ever since the last floods. Farmers, boatyard owners and the Haddiscoe Island residents fear that a Bure barrier would still result in flooding in the Yare Valley. Bob condemned the Haddiscoe Washlands scheme as 'harebrained' and doomed to failure, and, whilst admitting that a barrier on the Bure, coupled with washlands at Haddiscoe Island, would be the cheapest and least disruptive method to save some Broadland, he said 'Money doesn't come into it when you talk of drowning an island'.

37

Bob told me that the marshes in his youth were full of all kinds of birds. The marsh owners used to shoot geese on their land. Now the geese flocks have gone. 'Bertie High used to have an old brown dog; he used him like a fox,' recalled Bob. 'The dog would bring the geese over to Bertie hiding in a dyke, and he'd drown them'.

The R.S.P.B. now owns the Berney Arms side of the marshes. One of their officers asked Bob if he could inspect his marshes to find out the variation of species between the two different areas. Bob did not give him permission to walk over the marshes he manages, saying that a special duck, a garganey duck, was known to nest on his marshes rather than the R.S.P.B. ones 'because it didn't have a bloody camera always pointing up his arse!'

As I left Bob, a cluster of his associates from the cattle market joined him for a cup of tea and a mardle in the pub. This was his day out, he told me. He seemed to have plenty of friends - all of them working country people, weather-beaten and cheerful.

These men must be remembered and their skills passed on, because once these old traditions and crafts are lost they are never found again.

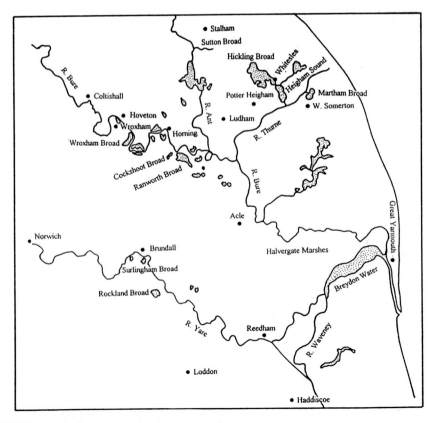

Steve and Michael Aldred

Thatchers

On a frosty day in early January, I went to Bengate Farm. The Aldred brothers were thatching the large barn. The frost was just melting on the ridge, and walking down the muddy lane I could see Steve and his brother Michael silhouetted against a cold grey sky, busily completing the last third of the ridge. Kneeling against a ladder each man was hammering the hazelwood brotches into position. The top 'fringe' of sedge was cut with a sharp thatching knife, and from a bundle lying to the thatcher's right, he selected the brotch and hammered it into position. With a deft movement sideways the ladder was jumped further along the roof, and the same traditional Norfolk triple diamond pattern of brotches was hammered over the sedge ridge.

Descending the ladders the brothers told me a little of their craft. 'The barn has been given a half thatch,' explained Steve. 'The north side needs repairing first. We're going on to the farm house next.' I was told that the sedge came from Somerton, cut by Richard Starling. 'We get a lot of our reed from him too,' explained Michael. 'At the end of the system the water is clear.' I asked what they looked for when buying reed. 'Straight, with strong stems and a good butt end,' both men agreed. They both

Sedge capping on Whiteslea's thatched roof

also thought that in general the reed beds were deteriorating, and the water quality was less good. 'Strong management is needed; the water level must be better controlled. The rivers are silting and the dykes often contain stagnant water. The reed beds are in a mess - too many vermin predators. We need keepers like in the old days to shoot the vermin. We have too many magpies, jays and harriers. Electrification of all boats is badly needed.'

'We've done our bit,' said both brothers. 'Father trained us.' Stephen, the elder brother had studied for two years at an agricultural college, and then worked on a pig unit. 'I wanted to set up my own pig farm, but with no capital, it was not possible to get started. With only seven thatchers twenty years ago, it seemed a good idea to follow in father's footsteps and carry on the family business.'

'There are too many men in thatching now,' interrupted his brother, 'well over thirty advertise. The boys do a short course in thatching, and T.A.S., the thatching advisory service, gets people started within six months, so the prices have come down, and there are many cowboys in the trade.'

Both men had a great love for their craft. 'I wished I had kept a portfolio of our jobs,' enthused Michael, 'but I have my memories of each job.' 'There is a great demand for good Norfolk reed,' said Stephen, 'and a future for the true tradesman, but people think what a romantic job it is - a rural idyll. In actual fact it is a hard physical job, especially bad on the back and the knees, as you spend a lot of time leaning against the roof on a ladder. People also want the job done immediately. Years ago, you could say "I'll come and do your job next year" - but now you have to thatch continuously just to pay off the mortgage. We both love to thatch, but do not enjoy the business side.'

Each man wore protective leather knee-pads, leather boots and used leggets that they made for themselves. 'You get used to the swing of it,' Steve explained, picking up his ash-headed legget and showing me its balance and how they hammered in the nail heads with which to butt the thatch. Both brothers were interested to examine old thatch, and to experiment and try out new methods. As it started to rain, the brothers explained that they couldn't thatch in wet weather, but ridging could be carried on.

Walking back to the North Walsham by-pass, and shivering in the gloom of that wintry day, my last glimpse of these well known thatching brothers, who got jobs by reputation and sheer pride and enthusiasm for their job, was to see them perched either side of the sixty-foot barn roof, one either side of the ridge, working their way along it. The physical stamina needed, the artistic eye and aesthetic sense ensures that those brothers are leaving behind a quality of workmanship for all to see for many years ahead. When they start on the farmhouse next month - after the rafters have been repaired - the existing thatch will be combed and patched, the moss removed, and finally the ridge replaced. 'That roof will then last another fifty years,' said Steve. After that they had to look at storm damage

Michael completing the sedge ridge on a barn

on a Tudor barn. 'We also like to work on new designs,' commented Michael, 'and to improve our standards, and in any case the sunsets are wonderful.'

George Newman, Eric Edwards, Richard Starling and Bob Mace might be scything, mowing and bunching the reed in the marshes this very month. Reed is cut every two years, in double swathes, in the autumn and winter when the sap is down and the leaves off the stems. Combing and cleaning the reed, and carrying the bundles out of the marshes on to the lighters to transport them on to the staithes to sell on, is work that has not changed much over the centuries. The sedge is cut green in summer months, and grows where there are old peat diggings. Again it is hard physical work, which does not attract sufficient younger men to train as apprentices to learn and continue these customs.

No wonder all the men I talk to in these jobs see a need for good back-up, and strong management to secure the future of Broadland's thatchers, marshmen and wardens on the nature reserves. Sadly, none of them are optimistic that Broadland marshes reed beds and wildlife will recover to good health unless persistent and strong management is secured. The satisfaction of the job, however, is plain to see in all these men. Another thatcher, Eric Edwards, said, 'It's hard graft. There's nothing easy about reed-cutting, particularly when there's a wind blowing, but it's very peaceful, when I mow in the old-fashioned way, just the swish of the scythe and the sounds of the fen.'

41

Jim and James Cole

Boatyard Owners

In the early 1950s a wife, maybe nostalgic for her Norfolk birthplace, suggested to her husband that they might holiday on a boat in Norfolk. They were engaged in running a furniture business in Surrey at that time. So successful was that wherry holiday, and such a good friend did the farmer owning the wherry become to Mr and Mrs Cole, that Jim asked about local property for sale. Norfolk and sailing very much appealed to him after his first visit to the county.

A riverside bungalow was bought in 1953. As part of the property deal, the *Liberty* wherry had to be bought as well. The price of the wherry was £900. The 1953 floods were especially bad that Christmas, and so the Cole family cooked their turkey in the flooded bungalow and passed it out to the floating *Liberty* where the Christmas lunch was enjoyed. Subsequently the *Liberty* was found to be faulty, and so the farmer friend insisted on returning £600.

'Tidecraft Cruisers' was begun as the Coles' new business venture, and together Jim and his wife Peggy built a boat shed. A Nottingham firm built Jim three two-berth cruisers, which was the basis of his fleet of hire boats. Shortly afterwards Jim employed a foreman to help build the boats. He bought *Arden*, a sixty-eight foot teak-built wherry and began to run wherry trips along the River Yare.

Jim remembered that an American colonel and his wife with lots of children were some of his earliest customers. 'I didn't know one end of a boat from the other,' he admitted, and as he turned the wherry round at Surlingham, he took the flesh off his knuckles and returned the wherry to his yard at Brundall in the pouring rain with a very bloodied fist. Next day the American family continued on the wherry trip down river towards Reedham. Peggy, who was pregnant at that time, and her eldest child James, ran the business whilst Jim was away skippering on that first wherry trip.

Eventually Jim owned three wherries, and his boat-building and hiring business flourished. James, the elder son, was seven when his parents moved from Surrey to Norfolk. He completed his education at Langley

The Cole family aboard their family wherry

School and, at the age of sixteen, left school and joined the family business, learning to build boats and run a business. Penny, Mr and Mrs Cole's daughter, worked for a solicitor originally, later owning and running a post office and general store at Neatishead. Eventually that was sold on, and she returned to her parents' home to establish a clothing boutique and fishing tackle shop besides the general store and marina. Simon, her son, works for his mother.

Flooding at Brundall on the banks of the River Yare is a constant problem. The house, boatyard andsheds are flooded each winter, if a spring tide and strong north-westerly wind happen to coincide. Jim Cole told me that his second daughter came home from abroad to visit her parents and had to sleep upstairs as the river flooded the downstairs bedrooms during her holiday. 'A Yare barrier is very necessary for us,' said a worried Mr Cole.

Looking back on a life in the boat-building business, Jim says, 'The winters are now the best.' Sitting in the cosy sitting room of Mr and Mrs Cole's elegant riverside house, which they had built in 1967, I could not help but agree. Outside, the bare trees, and the swirling tide of a grey river was peaceful and empty of traffic. Few people could boast such a lovely view from their lounge window. 'Customers that come on the boats are different too,' mused Jim, 'but some still want peace and beauty and come back time and time again to find it'.

Jim's son, James, now runs East Anglia's longest established brokerage. Norfolk Yacht Agency Ltd has provided service on the Norfolk Broads for the past twenty-five years. James, the founder of this business, clearly remembers his father's three wherries, the *Liberty*, the *Lorna Doone* and the *Arden*, and the wonderful family holidays he and his two sisters enjoyed on their parents' boating trips. Especially he recalls how clear the Broads water was when he and his sisters swam off the wherries. James inherited his father's love of a water-based life, and learned to enjoy hydroplane racing at Oulton Broad as a schoolboy. He competed successfully on a national level. 'I never considered anything else,' said James when discussing his career. 'Only boating interested me.' He confessed the hope that at least one of his three sons might want to join him in the business in due course.

The building side of the business has grown over the last two years. 'We built six this year,' reported a delighted James 'which was what we predicted. We are offering a range of Sovereign 34, which are produced by Bounty Boats. One has just been delivered to Lagos, to Tin Pan Island.'

At a recent London Boat Show at Earls Court, James Cole's stand, with its beautifully-presented cruiser on the pool, was one of the busiest in the Show. Business appears to be booming for the close-knit Cole family. 'We offer brokerage on all types of craft,' said James, 'and have a total of around seventy different boats. Our customers have therefore a lot of choice, and we can supply all the experience that they might need to deal with any type of craft.'

A Sovereign 34 from James Cole's modern fleet

George Newman

Reed-cutter

Two inches of rain fell last night, so I thought that it was likely I would find a reed-cutter off the marshes the following day. Enquiring in Hickling village where George lived, I was directed to 'the house with a bundle of twine hanging on the wall.'

George Newman, a big man with blue twinkling eyes and tanned complexion, invited me, a total stranger, into his small tiled cottage. When I left some two hours later I remembered to give him my name. 'Oh, I wondered who you were,' was the laconic comment of that contented, popular, self-made man.

His tiny neat sitting room had prominent photographs of his mother and brother on the bureau. There was an organised pile of laundry and a hoover in the corner. 'I look after myself,' he said waving towards them. I was told later that George calls in to see his brother daily 'to keep an eye on him!'

George told me a little about his childhood. He was the ninth of ten children. His father worked on a farm, later becoming a fisherman working on the drifters operating out of Great Yarmouth. His mother used to pull sugar beet and help in season in the fruit fields. George remembers his childhood as quiet and happy, enjoying rides on the Broad, first in reed lighters and then in a motor-boat called *Dun Shovin*. Lady Desborough giving summer parties on the lawn at Whiteslea to all the Hickling children was a highlight, as was the gift of a fishing rod which Jim Vincent bought for the boy. 'It cost him two bob,' recalled George.

When George left school at the age of fourteen he found seasonal employment at Cantley sugar beet factory and other farm work. The sea wall at Bacton needed building and that provided the next job. 'Two chaps on Horsey sands persuaded me to have a go at reed-cutting,' said George, 'so I went out with them in short wellies. I came home the next day and bought some long boots!'

George has carried on reed-cutting as a self-employed man ever since. He and 'Newks', his friend and companion, are the last two reed-cutters that still work the harvest by hand. Cutting, dressing and carrying the reed out of the beds is what George is well known for. 'In my prime I did

one hundred bunches a day,' he said without a hint of pride. He explained
how the reed is cut in a double whale, once every two years between
December and April when the sap is down, and the frost has stripped the
leaves off the stems. 'Reeds come stronger the second year; they need water
on them when they are growing. If the weather is dry for too long, grass
invades the beds,' he went on to explain.

When I asked him about his method of work, George told me that he
works from 8 a.m. until about 4.30 p.m., taking only a bottle of water on the
marshes with him. 'Three and a half hands go for a shoof of reed and six
shooves make up a fathom. The fathoms are sold in hundreds. The reed is
cut, thumped down on a draining board, dressed, combed to pull out the
rubbish, then bunched and tied with twine if the reed is dry enough,' he
explained. 'Easterly winds clear the water, but it stays muddy in the
south-westerlies,' I was told. 'I scythe with a crown-back scythe,' said
George. 'Don't like the riverbank scythe - it feels tinny. We do our own
handles.'

'You don't get crops of reed like you used to, but the reed around
Hickling is like steel; it's not so good on the marshes though.' Good
management on Horsey Estate had increased the crop quality but not the
quantity, and only by opening up the drains, letting the muck out, would the
reedbeds or ronds continue to provide the thatchers with the material they
needed. Foreign competition, particularly from the cheaper, less polluted reed
beds of Poland, was a cause for concern.

**George Newman
scything reeds -
hand-scything is
a dying craft**

Asked about poaching, George replied with a twinkle, 'I could tell you a lot, but I durs'nt.' However, I was told of the time when his dog caught a cock pheasant and some rabbits which had to be hidden beneath piles of agricultural gatherings as they unexpectedly passed a warden on the way home.

'You've never seen such mushrooms,' reminisced George, thinking back to the mid 70s when sheep were grazing the marshes. 'Those mushrooms were big as dinner plates after the sheep had been there - and the gravy you got too! You could get your food for the day off the marshes.' Sometimes though the shoe was on the other foot. He overheard somebody in the Nelson pub stating that he had thatched a new bird-table for his wife. When asked where he'd got the reed from, he overheard the explanation, 'Oh, I picked up a bunch or two off the staithe.'

George's reed-lighter

Sailing up to the council staithe at Hickling I had seen bunches of sedge left stacked up. After they had been there many weeks, blown about over the moored boats, rained on by the summer storms, and walked over by the holiday boat hirers, I asked George why they were left there. 'You can't teach someone to cut sedge in a day,' he commented drily. 'The wrong person was used to help out. The sedge was gabbled up, but tied too loosely. It had to be untied, combed free of rubbish and weed, and then retied.' I gather that thatchers, coming to pick up the sedge, had refused to buy it.

I learned from George that pliable sedge, used to cap the ridges over thatched roofs, is cut green between June and early September and is usually left a day to dry before being bunched and gabbled up and tied with a half-hitch. Sedge is usually priced at ninety pence a bunch and sold by the score of bunches. Sedge grows where old peat diggings had been and it is cut on three to four-year cycles. If sedge is left uncut, it will be invaded by carr, a tangle of buckthorn, alder and guelder rose. 'Sedge is killed if it is run over by box-cutters, and then reed will take over,' said George.

I was told, between peals of laughter, of the time when he and his friend were quanting sedge across Horsey Broad in half a gale, when they punted into holes of water, as the bales were blown off the lighter; and of another time when a Seagull outboard engine, being used on a boat moving reed bundles, still kept running after the boat had sunk.

Apart from reed-cutting, George's main interest in life is his sport. 'I played football until I was forty-five and tennis until I was fifty,' he said. He showed me a bag full of trophies, telling me that he now plays bowls, darts, and snooker in the village.

Showing me out of the cottage, George walked down the untended garden; at the gate he picked up a bag of apples. 'Gerald has called,' he said, then went back into his neat little kitchen to prepare his cockle lunch.

~~~~~~

Jim Vincent instructing his sister, Ida, in a gun punt, 1927

Ida Grosvenor and Betty Spooner.

Champion Shots

Ida Grosvenor, born in 1892 in Hickling, was the daughter of Robert Vincent, a fanatical game, clay-pigeon, and wildfowl shot who made his living as an eel-catcher and fisherman on the Norfolk Broads. His son Jim Vincent, brother of Ida, was probably the most famous Broadsman of all time. His bird-watching, wildfowling and fishing in the 1930s earned him a national reputation. Ida's talent with guns was noticed very early. When only five years of age she picked up her father's walking-stick gun, slipped a .410 cartridge into position, snapped home the breech, and shot a pigeon in the garden. The gun cupboard was kept locked after that. However, her spectacular shooting career spanned the next half century.

Always an independent girl, Ida learned to quant and sail on Hickling Broad, and by the age of fourteen was regularly taking part in the male-dominated sport of coot shooting, coverts and rough shooting and fowling. She attended the local school at Hickling, and in due course married, having met her husband as he travelled to Norfolk for a challenge shooting match with her father. There was a twenty-three year difference between her husband, a Londoner, and herself. 'We talked shooting every day of our marriage,' she once said, adding, 'We were called "that Pigeon pair".' Her husband was an all-round sportsman, equally at home with rifle and shotgun, winning two Olympic bronze medals and one silver with the latter.

1912 Stockholm - silver. 1920 Antwerp - bronze. 1924 Paris - bronze

Ida joined in all the activities that her husband's shooting parties activated, and there was a steady stream of the rich, famous and talented at the clays, the duck and the pheasant shoots. Amundsen of the South Pole epic watched Ida shooting and she also met the Emperor of Japan and King George V. Her shooting triumphs which she attributed to growing up within a fanatical shooting family, having many opportunities to train, and an ice-cool, unflappable, competitive nature, were many. She won the British Ladies D.T.L. Championship twenty-two times, broke clays all over Europe, won innumerable competitions, and more than held her own in a tough and highly competitive man's world.

Possibly she will be remembered most for taking part in the 1936 Berlin

Olympics. One hundred and forty men and Ida took part. She was placed sixty-third, and she won two prizes.

Many albums, newspaper cuttings, and beautiful trophies are kept by Betty Spooner, Ida's daughter, at the Hickling cottage where Ida spent her final years, looked after by her daughter. In the same row of cottages was the home of Jim Vincent. Ida and her husband retired from London to their Norfolk holiday home in 1946.She took her last title at the age of fifty-six years in 1949, but retired after the death of her husband. Her obituary in a local paper read: 'A gamekeeper's daughter who embarrassed many a male competitor with her prowess at clay pigeon shooting has died aged 97 years. She was a much-loved Veteran of Veterans who regularly shot with crowned heads, nobility, champions, and overseas visitors.'

Ida Grosvenor

Betty Spooner remembers the journeys to and fro from London to Hickling - catching the London train to Catfield where they would be met by an oil-lamp-lit pony and trap. In the cosy cottage were many memories of her famous mother. Albums full of photographs and cuttings from a wide range of newspapers including *The Illustrated Sporting and Dramatic News* were shown to me. As one would expect from such an unusual family, Betty too revealed herself as a personality one is glad to have met. 'She talks to everyone,' her husband once said, 'Betty would not only talk to a sack of potatoes, she would address each one individually.'

So as the evening light, glowing off the marshes and nearby Hickling Broad, lit up the pictures and trophies in the lounge, highlighting a past life, Betty entertained me with stories of her own past. She and her brother went to the local Hickling school until a scholarship took her to the Norwich Blyth school where she lived in digs from the age of eleven years, because her father, having lost money in the 1920s slump returned with his wife to London. 'I had quite a chequered career, but it's done me no harm and it taught me to be independent,' said Betty, still a lively, positive lady now in her late seventies.

During the second world war Betty, working in London in a department of the I.C.I., was sent out into the country. Anybody with a gun or rifle was asked to join up and help with the Local Defence. Betty queued up at the local police station. 'We didn't expect ladies to volunteer,' said the local police. 'You have ladies here with guns and experience, which is more use than men with none of these things,' replied Betty. Her name was reluctantly taken by the police and on returning to her typing, the local press rang asking for pictures and a story on her shooting abilities.

Betty and her brother had been well taught by their mother, and Betty became a leading clay shot in her own right. After being the youngest competitor in a London Clay Pigeon championship, and winning top prizes, she was featured on the Pathé News. 'They cut out the bits in the film when I missed,' said a chuckling Betty. She married an antique dealer and they enjoyed a very happy marriage. Her husband's ill heath forced them to leave London, but an attempt to set up an antique business in Hove on the South Coast also had to be abandoned after three years because the sea air was too damp. Their marriage was short, only nine years. When her husband died Betty said, 'Some people never know the meaning of happiness. If you love somebody enough you have to let them go.'

Betty, living on in her 'spiritual home', the Hickling cottage, described with enthusiasm her recent trip to America in her late seventies. She had never flown before, but she wanted to visit her cousins and she undertook the trip alone. 'I talked to the Captain for over an hour during the flight,' she enthused, then went on to describe the 'fairyland of light on the ice mountains' as the plane approached Portland.

Betty Spooner

51

Peter Bower

Wherry Fleet Owner

Late on the tide, *Wanderbug* and I returned from a few days cruise along the river Yare. Creeping into Surlingham Broad as the wind died and the tide turned, I put down a mud weight, rolled my boat tent over *Wanderbug* and prepared supper. A wherry mast and single sail just visible over the tops of the trees glided on to the broad. Supper was forgotten for the elegant lines of a wherry yacht was a very exciting sight. The *Olive* sailed up and down the broad, and despite the lack of wind, her huge white sail gathered sufficient breeze to keep her moving. Two other wherries followed, and like graceful swans, the trio disappeared off the broad.

Next morning, rowing off Surlingham Broad to pull out at Coldham Hall S. C. slipway, I caught sight of two wherries disappearing round a bend in the river. Peter Bower skippering the *Hathor* was the last to leave from their overnight berth at Coldham Hall quayside. With the unhurried movements of a professional sailor, single-handedly he cast off and pulled in his mainsheet and slipped down the river, but not before he told me that the three wherries were on their way to pick up guests at Reedham, as part of the Broads Authority week of celebrations of Norwich 800. 'See you in November when we are less busy,' invited Peter, as he and the wherry disappeared on the tide, slipping down the River Yare.

On a gale-swept wintry day months later I walked down a muddy lane towards the river at Wroxham and found large plastic sheet tilts over the wherries. Paul, a skipper I had met on an earlier school trip, allowed me to peep into *Hathor,* the last pleasure wherry which can be chartered today on the Norfolk Broads. It was built for Ethel and Helen Colman (daughters of the famous Norfolk mustard firm) and launched in 1905 at a cost of £2039-5s-4d. Possibly the name *Hathor*, who was the Egyptian goddess of love and joy, was chosen to commemorate their brother who died at an early age of tuberculosis whilst on a cruise on the Nile on her namesake the *Dahabeah-Hathor*. The *Hathor* was built by Mr D. S. Hall, a well known boat builder with a yard at Reedham. Walking around the oak and teak interior, it was a joy to see the interior light wood of sycamore with teak inlay of lotus flowers and Egyptian symbols of scarab, beetles, snakes, frogs and crocodiles in friezes on the door panels of the cabins. It was quite a shock to climb out of that Edwardian gentility back into the cold raw day of the 20th century - so ageless and beautiful was that wherry's interior.

Barney, a partner in the Wherry Charter Company, invited me to visit his wherry yacht the *Norada*. A man of seventy years, he climbed in and out of the stripped-out hull with the energy and enthusiasm of somebody half his age. He was concerned that the cabin should be dry, the mattresses aired and the bilges clean. *Norada* had been designed and built by Ernest Collins of Wroxham in 1912. She was named after a famous racing vessel of that time. She was chartered out until 1950 and then sold to a private owner. In 1964, the present owner, Barney Matthews, a former skipper at Ernest Collin's Yard, bought her.

In the wet berth behind *Norada* was *Olive*, again a wherry yacht with a counter (overhanging) stern on which one could relax in a deck chair on the extended deck space whilst the crew sailed the wherry. The *Olive* was built in 1909.

More than two hundred wherries worked the 130 miles (200 km) of navigable rivers and medieval peat diggings which flooded to make the Broads, for over two hundred years. Fourteen of the forty broads are still open to boats, but many derelict wherry hulls have been sunk in various broads, or used to shore up banks and staithes. Railways and roads offered the water-borne traffic (carrying everything from reeds, timber, coal, city refuse, farm produce, passengers and animals, and even ice-blocks) a faster and easier journey, and by 1949 not one trading sailing wherry existed. A few continued to work as motor barges with diesel engines fitted. The *Albion* wherry, built in 1898, was bought, refitted and re-rigged in October 1949. She carried cargo for some years more and now she carries passengers. The Norfolk Wherry Trust works hard to keep the last ever `Black Sailed Trader' active.

In the late 1950s *Hathor* was sold to Martham Boatbuilding and Development Company. From 1974 she sat de-rigged with no mast, serving only as a houseboat hired to summer holiday-makers. Eventually the Wherry Yacht Charter Company, who were providing Edwardian-style holidays on the Broads from their base at Wroxham, bought her for £13,500. After thousands of pounds spent in restoration over a period of nearly two years, she was added to the fleet of hire wherries. The fact that sycamore wood, which is very prone to warp, wood-worm and rot, was used inside *Hathor,* making restoration even more difficult, speaks volumes for the enthusiasm and quality of workmanship of Peter and Barney, who already worked their wherry yachts the *Olive* and the *Norada.*

The Wherry *Hathor* **at Thurne**

Photo: Matthew Dane

Peter Bower wrote: 'In September 1986 we pulled *Hathor* out on our slipway at Wroxham and began restoration of the hull. The planking appeared sound but we had to replace twenty-one of the 4" oak frames in whole or part, which involved stripping out most of the interior of the wherry . . .' *Hathor* started work in April 1988, one year later, to coincide with the new national park status for the Broads. Wherry Yacht Charter and the Broads Authority re-staged *Hathor's* launch ceremony at Reedham with descendants of the people who had attended the original launch mixing with the modern reconstruction boat workers.

'Tea Up!' called Chris, an apprentice with the firm. 'He's probably the only wherry apprentice in the world,' said Peter with a slow smile of approval as he passed me a mug of tea. I sat in their office as the men had their tea-break; their enthusiasm for the boats shone through the laid-back conversation. Peter had been a full time teacher in a Norfolk High School until he turned full time wherryman some years ago, and Barney his partner, had been in engineering in the Midlands. Now they have a love-hate relationship with the wherries. 'It's a labour of love which is a year-round job,' they admitted cheerfully.

Peter was anxious to give credit to the support, both financial and moral, of the Broads Authority. A grant helped them establish Chris Bentley's wherry apprenticeship. Excellent education leaflets, work programmes and brochures had been designed and printed with help from the Broads Authority. Peter still teaches on a part time basis, and his interest in education, care for the environment and his discipline in running the small company were very evident on my short visit. Two brochures were given to me: one for schools, highlighting 'Educational trips with a difference' and suggesting that the cruise could be used as part of the National Curriculum, especially in subjects like geography, science, social history and environmental studies; the second brochure highlighted the holiday aspect of the charters. They were the best holiday brochures I have ever seen.

'The wherries were hired out an average total of eighteen weeks annually, but last year was a bad year for all boatyards,' said Peter. 'We must keep the old things going, but all they give you back is bruises.' Peter's laid-back approach belied his genuine enthusiasm. However, he was pleased to acknowledge the support and aid provided by the Norfolk Society as well as the Broads Authority. He said he had no time for the doom and gloom attitude over the Broads. 'They are being gradually restored by the Broads Authority, with clear water and good re-establishment of water plants now evident in Cockshoot Broad, with Barton Broad about to be pumped free of mud and sludge,' he continued. 'The tourism bit is only worrying if it gets out of hand, but I see less of the 1960s yobbish element on boats now. A better type of person is being encouraged on to the Broads with activities designed to make people more aware of the fragility of the area.'

Barney has had a lifetime considering such issues. He was adamant that the Yare barrier should not be built. 'The flat flood meadows have absorbed the flood water for thousands of years,' he said. 'It is a natural process which cannot be stopped - banking too is useless.' He agreed with Professor Clayton of the University of East Anglia that coastal erosion cannot be stopped. 'The Dutch saved the Fens' said Barney dryly, 'but Eccles and other places down the coast were lost as a result. Boatyards have always flooded twice a year - and you must expect it. It's natural in this valley.'

Peter sees a wind of change on the Broads and thinks that the future is good. 'The get-rich-quick companies are going; there is a decline in bad behaviour on boats; people care more and the recreational and tourism department is being handled sensitively by the Broads Authority - they listen to you!' he said appreciatively.

Then the four men, Paul, part-time skipper, the two partners, Peter and Barney, and the apprentice Chris, discussed the technique that Nat Bircham's daughter used when helping out on the pleasure wherry cruises last season. Nat Bircham was the last professional wherryman. He owned the *Ella* and worked the *Albion* until 1991 and his daughters must have grown up watching the ways of their father's sailing techniques.

The Wherry Yacht Charter Company is one that is knowledgeable, hard working and anxious to allow the modern holiday-maker to experience a bye-gone age when Edwardians might have passed the evenings playing a piano in a cabin lit by candles or oil lamps, going to bed to the lullaby of wind whispering in the reeds or the hooting of the owl and the boom of the bittern.

A few modern holiday-makers may have read the earlier record of the original launch of the *Hathor*, as recorded by Humphrey the son of Florence Boardman. 'It was a lovely day at Reedham in July 1905, when the launching ceremony took place. The ladies wore their summer best, ankle-length frilly dresses with lace collars and leg-of-mutton sleeves. Some wore flat-topped white yachting hats, while the elderly were in black, their parasols shading their eyes. The menfolk were smart, Father was in white and the head-gear varied from boaters to bowlers, while the junior employees of Mr Hall wore caps . . . .'

Skipper and steward, who attended to every need of the earlier holiday-makers, have now been replaced by the modern hirer on a self-catering cruise accompanied by a skipper, but the Broads are as magical now as they were then, offering freedom, loneliness and awareness of nature.

19th century wherries at a Broadland staithe
(by kind permission of Mr & Mrs Holmes of How Hill)